Pp

Kelly Doudna

Published by SandCastle™, an imprint of ABDO Publishing Company, 4940 Viking Drive, Edina, Minnesota 55435.

Printed in the United States.

Cover and interior photo credits: Corel, Digital Stock, Eyewire, PhotoDisc, Rubberball Productions

Library of Congress Cataloging-in-Publication Data

Doudna, Kelly, 1963-
    Pp / Kelly Doudna.
        p. cm. -- (The alphabet)
    ISBN 1-57765-436-6 (hardcover)
    ISBN 1-59197-016-4 (paperback)
    1. Readers (Primary) [1. Readers] I. Title.

PE1119 .D685 2000
428.1--dc21

                                                                00-056898

The SandCastle concept, content, and reading method have been reviewed and approved by a national advisory board including literacy specialists, librarians, elementary school teachers, early childhood education professionals, and parents.

Let Us Know

After reading the book, SandCastle would like you to tell us your stories about reading. What is your favorite page? Was there something hard that you needed help with? Share the ups and downs of learning to read. We want to hear from you! To get posted on the ABDO Publishing Company Web site, send us email at:

sandcastle@abdopub.com

About SandCastle™

A professional team of educators, reading specialists, and content developers created the SandCastle™ series to support young readers as they develop reading skills and strategies and increase their general knowledge. The SandCastle™ series has four levels that correspond to early literacy development in young children. The levels are provided to help teachers and parents select the appropriate books for young readers.

Emerging Readers
(no flags)

Beginning Readers
(1 flag)

Transitional Readers
(2 flags)

Fluent Readers
(3 flags)

These levels are meant only as a guide. All levels are subject to change.

To see a complete list of SandCastle™ books and other nonfiction titles from ABDO Publishing Company, visit **www.abdopub.com** or contact us at:
4940 Viking Drive, Edina, Minnesota 55435 • 1-800-800-1312 • fax: 1-952-831-1632

Polly paints for fun.

Pat and Pam make pies.

Patty holds a pretty pie.

Paula snaps a picture.

Paul snips paper
with help.

Pete helps pick
peaches.

Pedro wears a striped shirt.

Ping plays in the park.

What does Peggy play?

(piano)

Words I Can Read

Nouns

A noun is a person, place, or thing

fun (FUHN) p. 5
help (HELP) p. 13
paper (PAY-pur) p. 13
park (PARK) p. 19
peaches (PEECH-ez) p. 15
piano (pee-AN-oh) p. 21
picture (PIK-chur) p. 11
pie (PYE) p. 9
pies (PIZE) p. 7
shirt (SHURT) p. 17

Proper Nouns

A proper noun is the name
of a person, place, or thing

Pam (PAM) p. 7
Pat (PAT) p. 7
Patty (PAT-ee) p. 9

22

Paul (PAWL) p. 13
Paula (PAWL-uh) p. 11
Pedro (PAY-droh) p. 17
Peggy (PEG-ee) p. 21
Pete (PEET) p. 15
Ping (PING) p. 19
Polly (POL-ee) p. 5

Verbs

A verb is an action or being word

does (DUHZ) p. 21
helps (HELPSS) p. 15
holds (HOHLDZ) p. 9
make (MAKE) p. 7
paints (PAYNTSS) p. 5
pick (PIK) p. 15
play (PLAY) p. 21
plays (PLAYZ) p. 19
snaps (SNAPSS) p. 11
snips (SNIPSS) p. 13
wears (WAIRZ) p. 17

23

More **Pp** Words

panda

penny

pirate

popcorn

24